j523.1   Bendick, Jeanne.
BEN
          The universe: think
          big!

$11.90

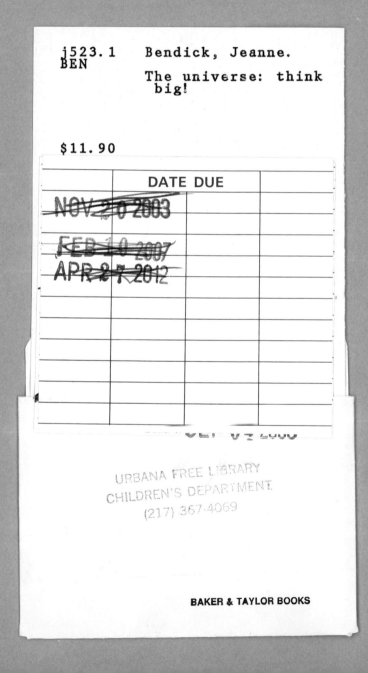

THE
Universe
THINK BIG !

An Earlybird Book
by Jeanne Bendick

Illustrated by Lynne Willey and Mike Roffe

THE MILLBROOK PRESS INC.

BROOKFIELD, CONNECTICUT

Cataloging-in-Publication Data

Bendick, Jeanne
The Universe, think big!
Brookfield, CT Millbrook Press, 1991.
32 p.; ill.: (Early Bird)
Includes index.
ISBN 1-878841-01-7   523.1   BEN
1.Universe   2. Outer Space   3. Galaxies

Text © 1991 Jeanne Bendick
Illustrations © 1991 Eagle Books Limited

Published by The Millbrook Press Inc, 2 Old Milford Road, Brookfield,
Connecticut 06804, USA

Produced by Eagle Books Limited, Vigilant House, 120 Wilton Road,
London SW1V 1JZ, England

Contents

The Universe

What is the biggest thing you can think of?
    An elephant?
    A skyscraper?
    Did you say the Earth?
    Did you say the Sun?

Can you think of something that's bigger than the Earth and bigger than the Sun?

Can you imagine something so big that nobody *knows* how big it is? Even scientists don't know.

The universe is bigger than anything you can imagine.

The Sun is part of it.

The planets are part of it, too.

So are all the stars.

So is all of space.

The universe is everything in space and all the empty spaces between those things.

The universe is everything there is.

Do you feel small and lost in all that space?

Your Address in the Universe

You are never really lost if you know your address.
Here's your address in the universe:

Your house
Your street
Your country
The continent you live on
Your planet, the Earth
The Solar System
Your galaxy, the Milky Way
The universe.

At night, when you look out into space, you can
see hundreds or thousands of stars. But you are
seeing only a very small part of the universe.

At night, when you look up at the stars, you
may not know it, but you are looking across great
distances in space.

Something About Distances

On Earth, a million miles is a very big distance. If you went around the Earth about forty times, you would travel a million miles.

In space, a million miles is a very short distance. Venus, the planet closest to the Earth, travels to within 26 million miles of us. In the universe, that's not even a giant step.

40 times around the Earth = 1 million miles

You know that to measure any distance you need a unit of measurement.

To measure a book, you would use inches.

To measure a room, you would use feet.

A football field is measured in yards, and distances between cities are measured in miles.

Distances in the universe are so big that even miles are too small to use. Really big distances need really big units of measurement. So, when they are measuring distances in the universe, scientists use a unit of measurement called a **light-year.**

A light-year is the distance light moves in a year.

Some galaxies are 800 billion light-years away.

To the nearest star, 4.4 light-years (26 million million miles).

15

How Fast Does Light Move?

Did you know that light moves?

When you turn on a lamp, light moves from the light bulb to your eyes. This happens so fast that it doesn't seem to take any time at all. The time is too short for us even to measure. But distances in space are so big that the time it takes for light to move from place to place *can* be measured.

It takes over eight minutes for the light from the Sun to reach Earth.

Too fast to tell

8 minutes

186,000 miles a second

In one second, light moves 186,000 miles.

In one year, light moves about 6 trillion miles. A trillion is a million million. Written out, it would look like this: 6,000,000,000,000. That's the unit of measurement called a light-year.

As far as anyone knows, nothing moves faster than light.

The fastest spaceship couldn't keep up with light for even a second.

Two Kinds of Measurement

A light-year measures two things.

It measures distance. "How far" is a measurement of distance.

It measures time. "How long" is a measurement of time.

Distance

93,000,000 miles

Time 8 minutes

18

How fast can you run?

If you say "50 yards," you're not giving the whole answer. If you say "15 seconds," you're not giving the whole answer either.

But if you say that you can run 50 yards in 15 seconds, that answers the question, "How fast?"

Six trillion miles a year is very fast.
But in the whole of the universe, one light-year is a very tiny amount.

Alpha Centauri is the star in the universe closest to our own star, the Sun. Alpha Centauri is about 4⅓ light-years away. If our Sun were the size of a dot, and you wanted to draw another dot to represent Alpha Centauri, you would have to draw it 10 miles away from the first dot.

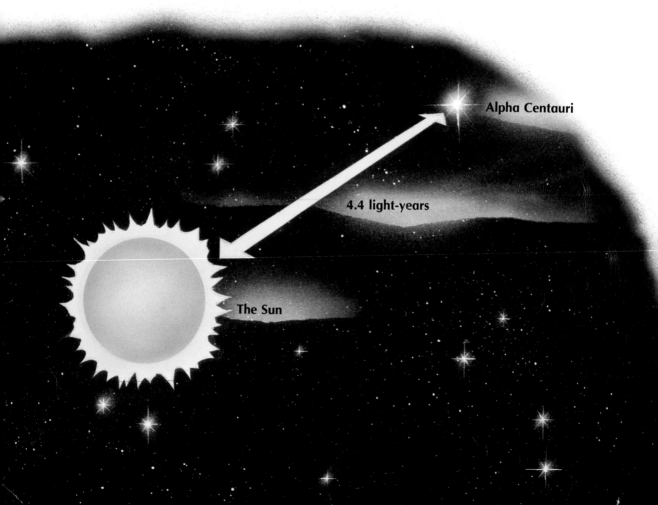

Alpha Centauri

4.4 light-years

The Sun

21

People didn't always know that the universe was so big. Once, they thought they could easily see all of it. They looked around and decided that the Earth was at the center of everything.

The Sun moved around the Earth.

The stars were fixed to the globe of the heavens.

At the center of everything the Earth stood still.

Is Seeing Believing?

If you believe only your eyes, you can see why people thought this.

The Earth certainly seems bigger than the Sun. But now we know that it is not.

The Sun appears to move around the Earth. It seems to rise in the morning. It seems to move across the sky all day. It seems to go down in the evening. But that's not what really happens. It is the *Earth* that is moving around the *Sun.*

The Earth seems steady under your feet. You can't feel it moving. But it's turning, and turning fast. Also, at the same time, it is swinging around the Sun.

It took a very long time for people to change their ideas. They were scared to change them. Who wanted to believe that they lived on a round ball that was spinning like a top and swinging through space?

Everything in the Universe Is Moving

The Earth spins.

All the planets in the Solar System spin, some fast, some slow. At the same time, they swing around the Sun.

Moons circle their planets.

Our Sun and billions of other stars make up a huge island of stars in space. This star island is called a **galaxy.**

There are billions of galaxies, many, many light-years apart from each other in space.

All the stars, planets, and moons in our galaxy, called the **Milky Way,** are turning together, like a giant wheel.

The Milky Way and all the other galaxies are speeding away from each other in all directions, across the universe.

As far as anyone knows, they may never stop moving. They may never reach the ends of the universe.

How Did the Universe Begin?

Nobody knows for sure, but here is what most scientists of today think.

Once, maybe 15 or 20 billion years ago, there was nothing but an incredibly small, hot (trillions of degrees), mysterious object. It probably wasn't made of any type of matter we know. It wasn't even energy as we know it.

Suddenly, this object exploded with a big bang.

Matter, energy, and space were created and flew out in all directions.

Scientists call this the **Big Bang theory.**

Over a million years, the matter formed into gases.

Over billions of years, it became galaxies, stars, planets, moons, and everything else in the universe.

As they have learned more, people have changed their ideas many times about how the universe began. There are still questions with the Big Bang theory. Maybe we will change our ideas again.

Index